Strategies for Effective Conflict Resolution in the Workplace

Olajide Adewale

Table of Contents

Introduction

In every workplace, conflicts are inevitable. They arise from diverse perspectives, varying workstyles, and the collision of personalities. While conflicts may seem disruptive and uncomfortable, they also present an opportunity for growth and positive transformation. Effectively managing and resolving conflicts is a critical skill that can lead to improved team dynamics, increased productivity, and a harmonious work environment.

"Strategies for Effective Conflict Resolution in the Workplace" is a comprehensive guide that equips individuals, managers, and organizations with the tools they need to navigate conflicts with confidence and competence. The writer examines the heart of workplace conflict, exploring its causes, impact, and potential for resolution. Through practical strategies, communication techniques, and real-life examples, readers will gain the knowledge and skills necessary to transform conflicts into opportunities for collaboration and growth.

This book is made of ten chapters, each addressing a crucial aspect of workplace conflict resolution. The initial chapters lay the foundation by explaining the nature of workplace conflicts and their root causes. It stresses the significance of proactive and constructive conflict management.

The subsequent chapters make deeper elaboration of the process of conflict resolution. They highlight the importance of effective communication, the various styles of conflict resolution, and a systematic approach to conflict resolution. Additionally, the book offers practical techniques such as active listening, managing emotions, and diffusing tension, which are essential tools for handling conflicts. It also discusses mediation and third-party involvement as effective conflict resolution methods.

Furthermore, the book explores strategies for dealing with difficult personalities and creating a conflict-resilient workplace culture. It also addresses challenges like power imbalances and persistent conflicts. Through this comprehensive guide, readers will be empowered to address conflicts proactively, communicate effectively, and implement strategies that promote positive resolutions. The principles and techniques presented in this book will foster a harmonious and productive work environment where conflicts are viewed as opportunities for growth and collaboration. Let *"Strategies for Effective Conflict Resolution in the Workplace"* be your guide to navigating conflicts with confidence, transforming workplace dynamics, and fostering a more resilient and cohesive team.

CHAPTER ONE

Understanding Conflict in the Workplace

Conflict is an inherent part of human interactions, and the workplace is no exception. While conflicts can often be perceived as negative or disruptive, they also present an opportunity for growth, learning, and positive change. In this chapter, the focus is on the nature of conflict in the workplace, its various dimensions and the impact it can have on individuals and organizations.

1.1 The Nature of Workplace Conflict

Workplace conflict can arise from a variety of sources, including differences in opinions, values, work styles, and personal backgrounds. Conflicts may manifest as disagreements over ideas, competition for resources, or clashes between different departments or teams. Conflicts can also stem from miscommunications, misunderstandings, or failure to meet expectations.

Conflicts can be overt, with visible disagreements and heated arguments, or covert, where tension and resentment simmer beneath the surface. In some cases, conflicts may be individual-based, involving personal issues between colleagues, while in others, they may be systemic, originating from organizational structures or policies.

Understanding the nature of workplace conflict is essential for effectively addressing and resolving it. By recognizing the root causes of conflicts, individuals and organizations can adopt proactive approaches to prevent conflicts from escalating and cultivate a culture that encourages open communication and constructive resolution.

1.2 Types and Causes of Workplace Conflict

Workplace conflicts can manifest in various forms, each with its unique characteristics and dynamics. Common types of workplace conflict include:

a. Interpersonal Conflict:

This type of conflict arises between individuals who may have clashing personalities, communication styles, or work methods. Differences in values, beliefs, and personal goals can also contribute to interpersonal conflicts.

b. Task-related Conflict

Task-related conflicts emerge when there are disagreements over work-related matters, such as project objectives, deadlines, or resource allocation. These conflicts are often centred around finding the most effective or efficient approach to completing a task.

c. Role Conflict

Role conflict occurs when individuals have conflicting expectations about their roles and responsibilities within the organization. This can happen when there are unclear job descriptions or when individuals are assigned tasks that may not align with their skills or expertise.

d. Organizational Conflict

Organizational conflicts arise from structural or systemic issues within the organization, such as a lack of clarity in reporting lines, inadequate communication channels, or conflicting departmental goals.

e. Value-based Conflict

Value-based conflicts occur when there is a clash between the fundamental values and beliefs held by individuals or groups within the workplace. These conflicts can be emotionally charged and challenging to resolve.

Understanding the different types and causes of workplace conflict enables individuals to identify conflicts early on and apply appropriate conflict resolution strategies based on the specific context.

1.3 The Impact of Unresolved Conflict

Unresolved conflict can have a significant impact on individuals, teams, and overall organizational performance and productivity. Some common consequences of unresolved conflict include:

a. Reduced Productivity

When conflicts remain unaddressed, they can lead to distractions, decreased focus, and a decline in overall productivity as employees become preoccupied with the conflict and unresolved issues.

b. Strained Relationships

Conflicts can strain relationships among team members, leading to decreased collaboration, trust issues, and a breakdown in effective communication.

c. Increased Stress and Morale Issues

Prolonged conflicts can create a tense and stressful work environment, affecting employee morale and job satisfaction.

d. Decline in Creativity and Innovation

Conflicts can stifle creativity and innovation as employees may be hesitant to share ideas or collaborate openly with those they are in conflict with. It is apt to note also that an innovative mind is a mind that is free of conflict and unresolved issues.

e. High Turnover Rates

Persistent conflicts can contribute to employee dissatisfaction and turnover, resulting in increased recruitment and training costs.

f. Negative Organizational Culture

A culture where conflicts go unresolved can foster a toxic atmosphere, inhibiting employee engagement and hindering the organization's growth and success.

CHAPTER TWO

The Importance of Effective Conflict Resolution

Having clarified the nature, types, and causes of conflict in the workplace as well as the impact of unresolved conflicts, in this chapter, we will explore the importance of addressing conflicts promptly and constructively, highlighting the significant role effective conflict resolution plays in promoting a harmonious and productive work environment. Indeed, understanding the impact of unresolved conflict emphasizes the importance of addressing conflicts proactively and implementing effective conflict resolution strategies.

2.1 Benefits of Addressing Conflict Promptly

One of the fundamental reasons for prioritizing effective conflict resolution in the workplace is to prevent conflicts from escalating and causing further damage. Addressing conflicts promptly offers several benefits, including:

a. Reduced Escalation

Early intervention in conflicts helps prevent them from spiralling into larger and more complex issues that may be challenging to resolve.

b. Improved Team Dynamics

Addressing conflicts promptly fosters a sense of trust and open communication among team members, leading to stronger and more cohesive teams.

c. Enhanced Productivity

By resolving conflicts quickly, employees can redirect their focus and energy back to their work, leading to increased productivity and efficiency.

d. Enhanced Creativity and Innovation

A conflict-free work environment encourages employees to share ideas and collaborate freely, fostering creativity and innovation.

e. Better Employee Morale

Addressing conflicts promptly and constructively contributes to a positive work culture, which, in turn, boosts employee morale and job satisfaction.

f. Reduced Employee Turnover

A supportive conflict resolution process reduces the likelihood of employees feeling undervalued or unappreciated, thus decreasing turnover rates.

2.2 The Role of Communication in Conflict Resolution

It is noted that most of the types and causes of conflict identified in the previous chapter are expressed in communication. Communication, therefore, stands as the cornerstone of effective conflict resolution. Open, honest, and empathetic communication helps parties involved in conflicts understand each other's perspectives, express their feelings, and seek mutually beneficial solutions. Key aspects of communication in conflict resolution include:

a. Active Listening

Active listening involves giving full attention to the speaker, seeking to understand their message, and showing empathy and respect for their feelings and viewpoints.

b. Clear and Constructive Expression

Encouraging individuals to express themselves clearly and constructively helps in articulating their needs and concerns without resorting to hostility or blame. An issue may sometime be resolved by merely allowing parties to express themselves thereon.

c. Collaborative Problem-Solving

Effective conflict resolution involves seeking win-win solutions through collaborative problem-solving. Encouraging parties to work together to find common ground promotes lasting resolutions.

d. Empathy and Understanding

Encouraging empathy and understanding allows individuals to step into each other's shoes, fostering a compassionate environment where conflicts can be addressed constructively.

2.3 Creating a Conflict-Resilient Workplace Culture

Building a conflict-resilient workplace culture is paramount in fostering effective conflict resolution. Organizations must prioritize open communication, trust, and emotional intelligence to create an environment where conflicts are seen as opportunities for growth rather than threats to be avoided. Some strategies for cultivating a conflict-resilient workplace culture include:

a. Providing Conflict Resolution Training

Offering conflict resolution training equips employees and managers with the skills and tools needed to navigate conflicts constructively.

b. Encouraging Mediation

Promoting mediation as a means of resolving conflicts encourages parties to collaborate with a neutral third party to find mutually agreeable solutions.

c. Establishing Clear Conflict Resolution Policies

Having well-defined conflict resolution policies helps employees understand the process for addressing conflicts and the available resources for support.

d. Leading by Example

Leadership plays a pivotal role in promoting a conflict-resilient culture. As they say, "Example is better than precept". When leaders demonstrate effective conflict resolution skills and communicate openly, employees are more likely to follow suit.

e. Recognizing and Celebrating Successful Conflict Resolution

Acknowledging and celebrating instances of successful conflict resolution reinforces the value of constructive conflict management within the organization.

CHAPTER THREE

Conflict Resolution Styles

Conflict resolution styles are the approaches individuals use to address and manage conflicts in the workplace. Each style is characterized by a distinct set of behaviours and attitudes, and understanding these styles is essential for individuals to adopt the most appropriate approach in different conflict situations. In this chapter, we will explore five common conflict resolution styles and their implications for workplace dynamics. By mastering these principles, individuals and organizations can navigate conflicts confidently and contribute to a positive and resilient workplace culture.

3.1 Collaborating: Seeking Win-Win Solutions

Collaborating is a conflict resolution style that prioritizes mutual understanding and cooperation. When individuals adopt a collaborative approach, they actively engage with the other party to identify common interests, share ideas, and jointly develop solutions that satisfy both parties' needs. This style is effective when the issue at hand is complex and requires multiple perspectives to arrive at the best outcome.

Key Characteristics:

- *Active listening and empathy*
  Collaborators are skilled at listening to others' viewpoints and demonstrating empathy, which fosters an environment of understanding and trust.

- *Open communication*
  Collaborators encourage open and transparent communication, allowing all parties to freely express their thoughts and concerns.

- *Creative problem-solving*
  This style involves brainstorming and exploring various options to find innovative solutions that address everyone's interests.

Benefits:

- *Fosters a positive work environment*
  Collaborative conflict resolution promotes teamwork and strengthens relationships among employees.

- *Builds trust*
  By acknowledging and respecting each other's perspectives, collaborators build trust and mutual respect.

- *Sustainable solutions*
  The solutions generated through collaboration are often sustainable and durable, as they consider the interests of all parties involved.

<u>*Challenges:*</u>

- *Time-consuming*
  Collaborative conflict resolution may take longer than other styles due to the effort required to reach a consensus.

- *Not suitable for urgent matters*
  In time-sensitive situations, collaboration might not be feasible, as it requires extensive communication and decision-making.

3.2 Competing: Asserting One's Position

Competing is a conflict resolution style in which individuals assert their own positions and prioritize their interests over others'. This style involves standing firm on one's viewpoint, using power and influence to achieve their goals, and may lead to a win-lose outcome, where one party gains at the expense of the other. This is common where one of the parties to the dispute has an upper hand or is superior or there is a greater cause, value or interest to uphold.

<u>*Key Characteristics:*</u>

- *Assertiveness*
  Individuals adopting a competing style are assertive in expressing their needs and advocating for their positions.

- *Goal-oriented*
  Competitors are focused on achieving their objectives and may be less concerned about preserving relationships.

- *Quick decision-making*
  This style can lead to quick resolutions, especially in situations that require decisive action.

<u>*Benefits:*</u>

- *Effective in emergencies*
  Competing can be effective in urgent situations where swift decisions are necessary to resolve critical issues.

- *Protects one's interests*
  This style can safeguard an individual's rights and prevent them from being taken advantage of in certain situations.

<u>*Challenges:*</u>

- *Strains relationships*
  The assertive and win-lose approach of competing may strain relationships and lead to resentment among colleagues.

- *Limited cooperation*
  This style may hinder opportunities for cooperation and collaboration, reducing teamwork and mutual support.

3.3 Compromising: Finding Middle Ground

The compromising conflict resolution style seeks to find a middle ground that partially satisfies both parties' interests. Individuals employing this style are willing to make concessions to reach an agreement and avoid an impasse. Compromising is often used when a quick resolution is necessary, and finding a mutually agreeable solution is more important than fully satisfying each party's needs.

Key Characteristics:

- *Willingness to give and take*
  Compromisers are open to making concessions and finding common ground to resolve the conflict.

- *Flexibility*
  This style requires individuals to be flexible in their demands and expectations.

- *Goal of maintaining relationships*
  Compromising seeks to preserve relationships by finding acceptable solutions for both parties.

Benefits:

- *Faster resolution*
  Compromising can lead to quicker conflict resolution as it involves finding a middle ground.

16

- *Preserves relationships*
  This style can help maintain positive relationships among colleagues, as it demonstrates a willingness to work together.

Challenges:

- *Partial satisfaction*
  Compromising may result in a solution that only partially satisfies both parties, leading to lingering dissatisfaction.
- *Potential for unsatisfactory outcomes*
  Compromising may lead to suboptimal decisions when a more creative or innovative solution was possible.

3.4 Accommodating: Yielding to Others

The accommodating conflict resolution style involves giving in to the demands or preferences of others, even at the expense of one's own interests. Individuals adopting this style prioritize maintaining harmony and relationships over asserting their own needs.

Key Characteristics:

- *Cooperation and adaptability*
  Accommodators willingly cooperate with others and adapt to their preferences.
- *Putting others first*
  This style involves prioritizing the needs and interests of others above one's own.

- *Preserving relationships*
  Accommodating is aimed at preserving relationships and avoiding conflict escalation.

Benefits:

- *Promotes goodwill*
  Accommodating can enhance goodwill and foster positive relationships, as it demonstrates a willingness to support others.
- *Reduces tensions*
  Yielding to others' demands can de-escalate conflicts and create a calmer working environment.

Challenges:

- *May lead to exploitation*
  In situations where one party consistently accommodates, it may create an imbalance of power and lead to exploitation by the other party.
- *Sacrificing one's interests*
  Accommodating too often can result in individuals neglecting their own needs and interests.

3.5 Avoiding: Temporarily Sidestepping Conflict

The avoiding conflict resolution style involves temporarily sidestepping the conflict without addressing it directly. Individuals using this style may avoid confrontation, hoping that the conflict will resolve itself over time or that the situation will change naturally.

<u>*Key Characteristics:*</u>

- *Conflict avoidance*
  Avoiders may minimize or deny the existence of conflicts to maintain peace.

- *Delaying action*
  This style involves postponing conflict resolution, which may allow tensions to simmer and intensify over time.

- *Indifference*
  Individuals adopting this style may display indifference or detachment from the conflict.

<u>*Benefits:*</u>

- *Provides time for reflection*
  Avoiding can offer time for individuals to reflect on the situation before addressing the conflict.

- *Prevents immediate escalation*
  Avoiding conflicts can prevent immediate escalation and offer time for emotions to cool down.

Challenges:

- *May lead to festering issues*
  Avoiding conflicts can allow underlying issues to fester and potentially escalate into larger problems.

- *Hinders growth and progress*
  Prolonged avoidance can hinder growth, cooperation, and the development of constructive solutions.

It is apt to note that understanding the various conflict resolution styles allows individuals to adapt their approach based on the specific conflict and desired outcomes. There is no one-size-fits-all approach to conflict resolution, and the most effective strategy depends on the circumstances of each case - nature of the conflict, the individuals involved, and the organizational context.

CHAPTER FOUR

The Conflict Resolution Process

The conflict resolution process is a structured approach used to address conflicts in a systematic and constructive manner. By following a defined process, individuals can effectively navigate conflicts and work towards mutually acceptable solutions. In this chapter, we will explore the key steps involved in the conflict resolution process, empowering individuals and teams to approach conflicts with clarity and confidence. Armed with these insights, individuals and organizations can navigate conflicts confidently and contribute to a positive and resilient workplace culture.

4.1 Step 1: Identifying the Conflict

The first step in the conflict resolution process is to identify and acknowledge the presence of a conflict. Sometimes conflicts may be overt and readily apparent, while at other times, they may be subtle or hidden beneath the surface. It is essential to recognize conflicts early on to prevent them from escalating and causing further damage.

Key Actions:

- *Listen to concerns*
  Actively listen to individuals involved to understand their perspectives and identify any underlying issues or tensions.

- *Observe behaviours*
  Pay attention to changes in behaviour, communication patterns, or performance that may indicate the presence of a conflict.

- *Encourage open communication*
  Create a safe and supportive environment that encourages individuals to express their concerns and discuss conflicts openly.

4.2 Step 2: Understanding Individual Perspectives

Once the conflict is identified, the next step is to gain a comprehensive understanding of each individual's perspective. Different parties involved may have different needs, interests, and viewpoints, which contribute to the conflict.

Key Actions:

- *Practice active listening*
  Give each individual the opportunity to express their thoughts, feelings, and concerns without interruption.

- *Ask clarifying questions*
  Seek clarification to fully understand the root causes of the conflict and the emotions involved.

- *Avoid assumptions*
  Refrain from making assumptions about others' motivations or intentions, and instead focus on understanding their perspectives.

4.3 Step 3: Seeking Common Ground

In this step, the focus shifts towards finding common ground and areas of agreement between the conflicting parties. Identifying shared interests can pave the way for collaborative problem-solving and mutually acceptable solutions.

Key Actions:

- *Identify common goals*
  Look for shared objectives or common values that both parties can align with.
- *Explore shared interests*
  Identify areas where the interests of both parties overlap or complement each other.
- *Highlight shared values*
  Emphasize shared values that can serve as a foundation for understanding and cooperation.

4.4 Step 4: Generating Possible Solutions

Once common ground is established, the next step is to generate potential solutions to address the conflict. Encourage brainstorming and creative thinking to explore a range of possibilities.

<u>*Key Actions:*</u>

- *Promote inclusivity*
  Involve all parties in the solution-generation process to ensure that diverse perspectives are considered.

- *Encourage creativity*
  Create an environment that encourages individuals to think outside the box and explore innovative solutions.

- *Evaluate pros and cons*
  Assess the feasibility and potential outcomes of each solution to determine their viability.

4.5 Step 5: Selecting and Implementing Solutions

After generating potential solutions, the conflicting parties must agree on the most suitable approach and implement the chosen solution. It is essential to ensure that all parties are committed to the agreed-upon solution and are willing to cooperate in its implementation.

<u>*Key Actions:*</u>

- *Reach consensus*
  Facilitate discussions to achieve a consensus on the selected solution among all parties involved.

- *Establish a timeline*

  Define a timeline for implementing the solution and outline the specific actions required.

- *Monitor progress*

  Regularly assess the progress of the solution's implementation and make adjustments as necessary.

4.6 Step 6: Evaluating the Resolution

The final step in the conflict resolution process involves evaluating the effectiveness of the resolution. This step allows individuals and teams to reflect on the outcomes and make any necessary adjustments for future conflict resolution.

Key Actions:

- *Reflect on the process*

  Evaluate how the conflict resolution process was conducted, considering what worked well and what could be improved.

- *Assess the outcomes*

  Determine whether the chosen solution effectively addressed the conflict and whether it had any unintended consequences.

- *Learn from the experience*

  Use the conflict resolution experience as an opportunity for growth and learning to improve future conflict resolution efforts.

By following a structured conflict resolution process, individuals and organizations can approach conflicts with a clear roadmap, ensuring that conflicts are addressed constructively and that solutions are reached in a timely and effective manner. The conflict resolution process empowers individuals to navigate conflicts with confidence, fosters collaboration and trust among team members, and contributes to a positive and harmonious work environment.

CHAPTER FIVE

Effective Communication for Conflict Resolution

Effective communication is the backbone of successful conflict resolution. When individuals engage in open, honest, and empathetic communication, they create a conducive environment for understanding, collaboration, and finding mutually acceptable solutions. In this chapter, we will explore the essential communication techniques and strategies that contribute to effective conflict resolution.

5.1 Active Listening

Active listening is a fundamental skill in conflict resolution. It involves giving full attention to the speaker, understanding their message, and demonstrating empathy and respect for their feelings and viewpoints. When individuals feel heard and understood, they are more likely to be receptive to finding common ground and resolving conflicts constructively.

Key Elements of Active Listening:

- Maintain eye contact and open body language to show that you are engaged in the conversation.
- Avoid interrupting the speaker and allow them to express their thoughts fully.

- Paraphrase and summarize the speaker's points to ensure clarity and demonstrate understanding.
- Use empathetic statements to acknowledge the speaker's feelings and emotions.
  Example: *"It sounds like you're feeling frustrated because your ideas were not considered in the project planning process."*

5.2 Clear Expression of Needs and Concerns

Effective conflict resolution involves individuals expressing their needs and concerns in a clear and constructive manner. Clear communication helps avoid misunderstandings and ensures that all parties are aware of each other's perspectives.

Key Tips for Clear Expression:

- Use "I" statements to express feelings and concerns without blaming others.
- Be specific about the issues at hand, providing concrete examples to illustrate your points.
- Focus on the behaviour or action rather than the individual's character.
- Avoid making assumptions and seek clarification when needed.
  Example: *"I feel overwhelmed when I'm assigned multiple tasks with tight deadlines, and I'm unsure how to prioritize them. I would appreciate some guidance on managing my workload effectively."*

5.3 Managing Emotional Triggers

Conflicts can evoke strong emotions, which may hinder effective communication and problem-solving. It is essential to manage emotional triggers to maintain a constructive atmosphere during conflict resolution discussions.

Key Strategies for Managing Emotions:

- Practice deep breathing and self-regulation techniques to stay calm during heated discussions.

- Take a break if emotions are running high, allowing time to cool down before resuming the conversation.

- Recognize that emotions are natural but try to focus on the issue at hand and avoid personal attacks.
  Example: *"I understand that this situation is frustrating, and we may have different viewpoints. Let's take a short break and reconvene when we're both in a calmer state of mind."*

5.4 Reframing Negative Language

Language can significantly impact the tone and direction of conflict resolution discussions. By reframing negative language into more positive and constructive expressions, individuals can foster a more collaborative and solution-oriented atmosphere.

<u>*Key Tips for Reframing Language:*</u>

- Replace accusatory language with neutral and non-blaming statements.

- Focus on expressing needs and interests rather than dwelling on past mistakes.

- Use language that invites collaboration and problem-solving.
  Example: Instead of saying, *"You never listen to my ideas,"* reframe it to, *"I would appreciate more opportunities to share my ideas during team meetings."*

5.5 Emphasizing Solutions and Common Goals

During conflict resolution discussions, it is vital to shift the focus towards finding solutions and identifying common goals. By highlighting areas of agreement and potential win-win outcomes, individuals can work collaboratively to address the conflict.

<u>*Key Strategies for Emphasizing Solutions:*</u>

- Brainstorm potential solutions together and evaluate each option's pros and cons.

- Emphasize shared interests and goals to foster a sense of cooperation.

- Encourage a problem-solving mindset rather than dwelling on the conflict's history.
  Example: *"While we may have different approaches, our common goal is to complete the project successfully.*

Let's explore options that combine our strengths to achieve this."

5.6 Seeking Mediation or Third-Party Involvement

In cases where direct communication between conflicting parties becomes challenging, seeking mediation or involving a neutral third party can facilitate constructive communication and help find a resolution.

Key Considerations for Mediation:

- Choose a mediator who is trained in conflict resolution and remains neutral throughout the process.
- Ensure that all parties involved agree to the mediation process and are committed to finding a resolution.
- Allow the mediator to facilitate communication and guide the discussion towards a mutually acceptable solution.
  Example: *"Given the complexity of this issue, I believe involving a mediator could help us navigate the conflict more effectively. Are you open to exploring this option together?"*

Undoubtedly, where effective communication techniques are implemented, individuals can build a strong foundation for conflict resolution. Active listening, clear expression, managing emotions, and reframing language contribute to a positive and collaborative conflict resolution process. By emphasizing solutions and seeking external support when necessary, individuals can foster an environment that values open communication and constructive problem-solving. Over and above, effective communication empowers individuals to navigate conflicts with confidence, foster collaboration and trust among team members, and contribute to a positive and harmonious work environment.

CHAPTER SIX

Strategies for Diffusing Tension and Hostility

Tension and hostility can escalate conflicts and hinder productive conflict resolution. Diffusing tension is crucial for creating a safe and supportive environment where individuals can openly communicate and work towards resolving conflicts constructively. This chapter is centred on effective strategies for diffusing tension and fostering a positive atmosphere during conflict resolution.

6.1 Remain Calm and Composed

Maintaining a calm and composed demeanour is essential for diffusing tension during conflict resolution. When individuals remain composed, they set a positive example for others and create a space where emotions can be managed effectively.

Key Strategies:

- Practice deep breathing and mindfulness techniques to stay centred and composed.
- Avoid reacting impulsively to provocations and instead respond thoughtfully.
- Choose neutral body language and facial expressions to convey a sense of calmness.
  Example: *"I understand this is a challenging situation, and I want to address it in a calm and*

collected manner. Let's take a moment to breathe before continuing our discussion."

6.2 Use "I" Statements to Express Feelings

When expressing feelings and concerns during conflict resolution, using "I" statements can prevent sounding accusatory and promote open communication. "I" statements focus on personal experiences and emotions, facilitating a deeper understanding of each party's perspective.

Key Strategies:

- Start sentences with "I feel," "I think," or "I believe" to express thoughts and emotions.
- Avoid blaming or accusing others by refraining from using "you" statements.
- Be specific about the emotions you are experiencing and the impact of the conflict on you.
  Example: *"I feel frustrated when deadlines are not communicated clearly because it makes it challenging for me to plan and prioritize my tasks effectively."*

6.3 Practice Active Listening

Active listening is instrumental in diffusing tension and demonstrating empathy during conflict resolution. When individuals feel heard and understood, they are more likely to be receptive to finding common ground and working towards a resolution.

<u>*Key Strategies:*</u>

- Maintain eye contact and give your full attention to the speaker.

- Refrain from interrupting and allow the speaker to express their thoughts without judgment.

- Use verbal and non-verbal cues to show that you are actively listening, such as nodding and paraphrasing.
  Example: *"I hear what you're saying, and I understand how important this issue is to you. Please continue sharing your thoughts, and I'm here to listen."*

6.4 Find Areas of Agreement and Common Ground

Identifying areas of agreement and common ground is a powerful strategy for diffusing tension and creating a sense of collaboration during conflict resolution. Emphasizing shared interests can lead to finding solutions that satisfy both parties' needs.

<u>*Key Strategies:*</u>

- Actively look for points of agreement, no matter how small they may seem.

- Acknowledge the validity of the other person's viewpoints and find areas of alignment.

- Highlight common goals and interests that both parties can work towards together.

Example: *"While we may have different approaches, it seems like we both value completing the project on time. Let's explore how we can merge our ideas to achieve this goal."*

6.5 Establish Boundaries and Respectful Communication

Setting clear boundaries for communication and promoting respectful discourse is essential for diffusing tension and maintaining a constructive atmosphere during conflict resolution.

Key Strategies:

- Agree on ground rules for communication, such as avoiding personal attacks or raising voices.

- Encourage a culture of respect where each person's viewpoints are valued and listened to.

- Be assertive in maintaining boundaries and addressing disrespectful behaviour promptly.
  Example: *"Let's agree to discuss our differing opinions respectfully and avoid making derogatory comments. This will help us focus on the issue at hand and work towards a solution together."*

6.6 Take Breaks When Needed

In emotionally charged conflict situations, taking breaks can be beneficial for diffusing tension and allowing individuals to cool down before resuming the discussion. Breaks provide an opportunity for reflection and self-regulation.

Key Strategies:

- Recognize when emotions are escalating and it's becoming challenging to communicate effectively.

- Suggest a temporary break to allow time for emotions to subside and clarity to be regained.

- Return to the discussion when all parties feel ready to engage constructively.
  Example: *"I can see that this conversation is becoming emotionally charged. Let's take a short break, and we can reconvene later when we're in a calmer state to find a resolution."*

It is evident in the manner of presentation of the foregoing that by implementing these strategies, individuals can effectively diffuse tension and hostility during conflict resolution. Remaining calm and composed, using "I" statements, practising active listening, finding common ground, establishing boundaries, and taking breaks when needed create a supportive environment for constructive communication and conflict resolution. These approaches empower individuals to navigate conflicts with empathy and respect, fostering collaboration and trust among team members, and contributing to a positive and harmonious work environment.

CHAPTER SEVEN

Mediation and Third-Party Involvement

Mediation and third-party involvement play a crucial role in conflict resolution, especially when direct communication between conflicting parties becomes challenging or unproductive. Mediators act as neutral facilitators, helping individuals work through their differences and find mutually acceptable solutions. Here, the writer takes you through the concept of mediation, the benefits it offers, and how to effectively involve a third party in resolving workplace conflicts.

7.1 What is Mediation?

Mediation is a structured and voluntary process where a neutral third party, known as a mediator, facilitates communication and negotiation between conflicting parties. The mediator does not have decision-making authority but instead guides individuals toward exploring their interests, identifying common ground, and generating potential solutions.

Key Features of Mediation:

- *Neutral Facilitator*
  The mediator remains impartial and does not take sides, ensuring a fair and unbiased process.

- *Confidentiality*
  Information discussed during mediation is typically kept confidential, creating a safe space for open communication.
- *Voluntary Participation*
  Mediation is a voluntary process, and all parties must agree to participate willingly.

7.2 Benefits of Mediation

Mediation offers numerous benefits for conflict resolution in the workplace. It provides a structured and collaborative environment for parties to work through their differences, fostering a sense of ownership over the resolution.

Key Benefits of Mediation:

- *Improved Communication*
  Mediators help individuals communicate more effectively and ensure that each party's perspective is heard and understood.
- *Empowerment*
  Mediation empowers individuals to be actively involved in finding solutions, promoting a sense of control over the outcome.
- *Preserves Relationships*
  Mediation focuses on finding win-win solutions, which can preserve relationships and reduce animosity among parties.

- *Time and Cost-Efficient*
  Mediation is often quicker and less expensive than formal legal proceedings, making it a cost-effective approach to conflict resolution.

- *Enforcement of Agreement*
  Where applicable, an agreement reached and properly executed following a mediation process can be enforced by an appropriate court of law.

7.3 When to Use Mediation

Mediation is particularly effective in various workplace conflict scenarios, including interpersonal conflicts, team disagreements, and misunderstandings that hinder collaboration.

Suitable Scenarios for Mediation:

- Disputes between colleagues or team members with differing perspectives or communication styles.

- Misunderstandings or conflicts arising from miscommunication or lack of clarity.

- Situations where individuals have been unable to resolve the conflict through direct communication.

- Employer and employees' union conflict situations.

7.4 Selecting a Mediator

Choosing the right mediator is critical to the success of the mediation process. The mediator should have a background in conflict resolution, communication skills, and the ability to remain neutral and unbiased.

Key Considerations for Selecting a Mediator:

- *Expertise*
  Look for a mediator with experience and training in conflict resolution, preferably with knowledge of workplace dynamics.

- *Neutrality*
  Ensure that the mediator is impartial and does not have any vested interest in the outcome.

- *Compatibility*
  The mediator should be someone all parties feel comfortable working with and trust to facilitate the process effectively.

7.5 The Mediation Process

The mediation process typically follows a structured approach to ensure a systematic exploration of the conflict and potential solutions.

<u>*Key Steps in the Mediation Process:*</u>

1. Introduction

The mediator introduces himself and explains the mediation process, including confidentiality and ground rules for communication.

2. Opening Statements

Each party is given an opportunity to express their perspective and outline their concerns without interruption.

3. Joint Discussion

The mediator facilitates a collaborative discussion, encouraging parties to explore common interests and areas of agreement.

4. Private Caucuses (If Needed)

The mediator may conduct private sessions with each party to delve deeper into their concerns and interests.

5. Generating Solutions

Parties brainstorm potential solutions and explore compromises that meet both parties' needs.

6. Agreement

If a resolution is reached, the parties draft a written agreement outlining the agreed-upon solutions and commitments.

7.6 Ensuring Mediation Success

To ensure a successful mediation process, all parties involved must approach the process with a commitment to active participation and a willingness to explore solutions.

Key Factors for Mediation Success:

- *Openness to Communication*
  Participants should be willing to listen to each other's perspectives and engage in constructive dialogue.

- *Flexibility*
  Parties should be open to exploring various solutions and compromises.

- *Accountability*
  Commitments made during mediation should be honoured and followed through.

Suffice it to say in view of the above analysis that by involving a neutral third party through mediation, organizations can effectively address workplace conflicts, promote understanding, and develop win-win solutions. Mediation empowers individuals to take an active role in resolving their conflicts, contributing to a positive and harmonious work environment. It is a valuable tool for creating a culture of open communication and collaborative conflict resolution within the workplace.

CHAPTER EIGHT

Navigating Difficult Personalities in Conflict

Dealing with difficult personalities during conflicts can be challenging and emotionally draining. Some individuals may have communication styles or behavioural tendencies that exacerbate conflicts, making resolution more complex. In this chapter, the effective strategies for navigating difficult personalities during conflicts and fostering constructive communication are demystified.

8.1 Recognizing Difficult Personalities

The first step in navigating difficult personalities is to recognize the traits and behaviours that make certain individuals challenging to work with during conflicts. Difficult personalities may exhibit traits such as aggressiveness, defensiveness, passive-aggressiveness, or an unwillingness to compromise.

Common Difficult Personality Traits:

1. Aggressiveness

Individuals who are confrontational, assertive, and tend to dominate conversations. It is noted that frustration triggers aggression. Thus, this trait may not be permanent or habitual to a party exhibiting it.

2. Defensiveness

People who are overly sensitive to criticism and may become defensive or reactive during conflicts.

3. Passive-Aggressiveness

Individuals who express their frustration indirectly through subtle, negative behaviours.

4. Avoidance

People who withdraw from conflict discussions and avoid addressing issues directly.

8.2 Maintaining Emotional Regulation

When dealing with difficult personalities, it is essential to maintain emotional regulation and avoid becoming entangled in their emotional responses. Emotional intelligence plays a crucial role in navigating conflicts effectively.

Strategies for Emotional Regulation:

- Take deep breaths and practice mindfulness to stay centred during difficult interactions.
- Reframe negative emotions as opportunities for growth and learning.
- Focus on the issue at hand rather than allowing personal feelings to influence the conversation.

8.3 Active Listening and Empathy

Active listening and empathy are powerful tools for disarming difficult personalities and fostering open communication. Demonstrating genuine interest in understanding the other person's perspective can de-escalate conflicts.

Techniques for Active Listening and Empathy:

- Give the individual your full attention and maintain eye contact to show that you are engaged.
- Reflect back their feelings and concerns to show understanding and validation.
- Avoid interrupting and allow them to express themselves fully.

8.4 Setting Boundaries

In dealing with difficult personalities, it is essential to establish and maintain clear boundaries for respectful communication. Boundaries help prevent conflicts from escalating further and maintain a productive atmosphere.

Steps to Set Boundaries:

- Politely but firmly assert your need for respectful communication during the conflict resolution process.

- Address any inappropriate behaviour immediately and request a change in approach.
- If necessary, take a break from the conversation to reset boundaries if they are crossed.

8.5 Reframing Language

Communication with difficult personalities can be fraught with negativity. Reframing negative language and choosing more constructive expressions can de-escalate tension and shift the focus toward finding solutions.

Techniques for Reframing Language:

- Refrain from using accusatory language and focus on specific behaviours or actions.
- Choose neutral and non-blaming language to convey your concerns and interests.
- Replace negative statements with positive alternatives to encourage a more collaborative tone.

8.6 Collaboration and Problem-Solving

Despite the challenges posed by difficult personalities, fostering a collaborative problem-solving approach can create an environment where conflicts are addressed constructively.

Strategies for Collaboration and Problem-Solving:

- Encourage the difficult individual to participate in brainstorming potential solutions.
- Emphasize shared interests and common goals to build a foundation for cooperation.
- Focus on finding win-win outcomes that satisfy both parties' needs.

8.7 Seeking Support

In some cases, dealing with difficult personalities may require seeking support from supervisors, HR professionals, or external mediators. Involving a neutral third party can help facilitate communication and promote an unbiased resolution.

When to Seek Support:

- When communication becomes unproductive or reaches an impasse.
- If the conflict has a significant impact on team dynamics or productivity.
- When attempts at direct resolution have been unsuccessful.

CHAPTER NINE

Cultivating a Conflict-Resilient Workplace

A conflict-resilient workplace is one that embraces conflicts as opportunities for growth, learning, and improved relationships. Rather than avoiding conflicts, a conflict-resilient workplace fosters an environment where conflicts are addressed constructively, leading to stronger teams and increased productivity. This chapter examines the strategies for cultivating a conflict-resilient workplace and creating a culture that values open communication, collaboration, and effective conflict resolution.

9.1 Promote Open Communication

Open communication is the foundation of a conflict-resilient workplace. When employees feel comfortable expressing their concerns, ideas, and feedback, conflicts can be addressed early on and prevented from escalating.

Key Strategies:

- *Encourage Two-Way Feedback*
  Create channels for employees to provide feedback to each other and to management regularly.

- *Foster a No-Blame Culture*
  Emphasize that conflicts are natural and that the focus is on finding solutions rather than assigning blame.

- *Conduct Regular Check-Ins*
  Schedule one-on-one meetings to allow employees to discuss any concerns or issues they may be facing.

9.2 Provide Conflict Resolution Training

Conflict resolution training equips employees and managers with the skills needed to handle conflicts effectively. Training sessions can cover topics such as active listening, empathy, negotiation, and collaborative problem-solving.

Key Strategies:

- *Customize Training Programmes*
  Tailor conflict resolution training to address specific workplace challenges and scenarios.

- *Include Role-Playing Exercises*
  Role-playing allows participants to practice conflict resolution techniques in a safe and controlled environment.

- *Offer Ongoing Support*
  Provide resources and support after the training to reinforce the learning and encourage its application in real-life situations.

9.3 Establish Clear Conflict Resolution Procedures

Having clear conflict resolution procedures in place ensures that conflicts are handled consistently and fairly. Employees should know how to initiate the resolution process and what steps will be taken to address their concerns.

Key Strategies:

- *Document Procedures*
  Put conflict resolution procedures in writing and make them easily accessible to all employees.

- *Include Multiple Avenues for Resolution*
  Offer various options, such as informal discussions, mediation, or involving HR, depending on the nature of the conflict.

- *Emphasize Confidentiality*
  Assure employees that their concerns will be handled confidentially to encourage them to come forward without fear of retaliation.

9.4 Encourage Collaboration and Team Building

Promoting collaboration and team building can strengthen relationships among employees, making it easier for them to address conflicts constructively.

Key Strategies:

- *Organize Team-Building Activities*
  Plan team-building exercises and activities to enhance team cohesion and trust.

- *Foster a Supportive Atmosphere*
  Encourage employees to support each other and work as a team to achieve common goals.

- *Recognize and Celebrate Achievements*
  Acknowledge and celebrate team accomplishments to foster a positive team spirit.

9.5 Lead by Example

Leaders and managers play a vital role in cultivating a conflict-resilient workplace. They must lead by example and demonstrate effective conflict resolution skills.

Key Strategies:

- *Show Vulnerability*
  Acknowledge that conflicts happen and share experiences of conflicts resolved positively.

- *Listen Actively*
  Demonstrate active listening when employees come forward with concerns, showing empathy and understanding.

- *Model Constructive Behaviour*
  Handle conflicts with professionalism and show respect for all parties involved.

9.6 Encourage Continuous Learning and Improvement

A conflict-resilient workplace values continuous learning and improvement. Employees should be encouraged to seek feedback, reflect on their conflict resolution experiences, and identify areas for growth.

Key Strategies:

- *Conduct Post-Conflict Reviews*
  After resolving conflicts, encourage employees to review the process and identify what went well and what could be improved.
- *Provide Opportunities for Skill Development*
  Offer workshops, seminars, or online courses on conflict resolution and related soft skills.
- *Celebrate Learning and Growth*
  Recognize and celebrate employees' efforts to improve their conflict resolution skills and handle conflicts constructively.

CHAPTER TEN

Overcoming Challenges in Conflict Resolution

Conflict resolution is a complex process that can present various challenges, ranging from emotional barriers to deeply rooted disagreements. Overcoming these challenges requires a combination of effective communication, empathy, and a commitment to finding common ground. In this concluding chapter, the writer points out the common challenges in conflict resolution and strategies to address them successfully.

10.1 Emotional Reactions and Bias

Emotional reactions can hinder effective conflict resolution, as individuals may become defensive, reactive, or overwhelmed by their feelings. Additionally, biases and preconceptions about the other party may cloud judgment and prevent open-mindedness.

Strategies to Overcome Emotional Reactions and Bias:

- *Practice Emotional Regulation*
  Encourage all parties involved to manage their emotions by taking breaks when needed and using techniques like deep breathing and mindfulness.

- *Foster Self-Awareness*
  Encourage individuals to reflect on their emotional triggers and biases to recognize how they may impact the conflict resolution process.

- *Engage in Perspective-Taking*
  Encourage each party to consider the other's perspective to develop empathy and understanding, helping to overcome bias.

10.2 Lack of Communication and Transparency

In some conflicts, individuals may avoid communication altogether or withhold information, making it challenging to address the underlying issues effectively.

Strategies to Overcome Lack of Communication and Transparency:

- *Create Safe Spaces for Communication*
  Foster an environment where individuals feel comfortable expressing their concerns without fear of judgment or retaliation.

- *Encourage Active Listening*
  Emphasize the importance of active listening to ensure that all parties feel heard and understood.

- *Practice Transparent Communication*
  Promote transparency by encouraging individuals to share relevant information and be upfront about their intentions and needs.

10.3 Power Imbalance

Conflicts between individuals with a significant power imbalance can be challenging to resolve, as the less powerful party may feel intimidated or reluctant to express his/her concerns or may feel that the resolution process would not be fair to him/her by virtue of his/her position or status.

Strategies to Address Power Imbalance:

- *Provide Neutral Mediation*
  Involve a neutral third party, such as a mediator, to level the playing field and create a safe space for communication.

- *Ensure Inclusive Decision-Making*
  Encourage participatory decision-making, where all parties have an opportunity to contribute to the resolution process.

- *Establish Accountability*
  Hold individuals with more power accountable for creating a supportive and respectful environment for conflict resolution.

10.4 Deep-Seated Disagreements

Some conflicts stem from long-standing disagreements and historical tensions, making resolution more complex.

Strategies to Address Deep-Seated Disagreements:

- *Focus on Common Goals*
  Identify shared interests and goals that all parties can work towards, even if there are fundamental disagreements.
- *Break the Issues Down*
  Address smaller, more manageable aspects of the conflict first, which may help build trust and pave the way for resolving more significant disagreements.
- *Emphasize Future Solutions*
  Instead of dwelling on past grievances, shift the focus towards finding solutions for the future.

10.5 Resistance to Change

Conflict resolution often requires some level of change or compromise, which can be met with resistance from individuals who are reluctant to adjust their positions.

Strategies to Overcome Resistance to Change:

- *Highlight the Benefits of Resolution*
  Emphasize the positive outcomes that can result from resolving the conflict, such as

improved teamwork, increased productivity, and enhanced relationships.

- *Involve All Parties in the Solution*
  Encourage each party to contribute to the resolution process and take ownership of the proposed solutions.

- *Be Patient and Persistent*
  Change takes time, and it is essential to be patient while working towards a resolution. Persist in finding common ground and maintaining open communication.

10.6 Escalation of Conflict

If conflicts are not addressed promptly, they can escalate and become more challenging to resolve.

Strategies to Prevent Escalation:

- *Address Conflicts Early*
  Encourage individuals to address conflicts as soon as they arise, rather than letting them simmer and worsen over time.

- *Establish Conflict Resolution Procedures*
  Ensure that clear and effective conflict resolution procedures are in place to guide individuals in handling conflicts promptly and constructively.

- *Provide Training on Conflict Management*
  Equip employees with the skills and knowledge needed to manage conflicts effectively to prevent them from escalating.

Conclusion

In *"Strategies for Effective Conflict Resolution in the Workplace,"* we embarked on a journey to transform workplace conflicts from obstacles into opportunities for growth and positive change. Throughout this book, we explored powerful techniques, practical approaches, and invaluable insights to equip you with the tools to navigate conflicts with finesse and confidence.

As we conclude this transformative expedition, we hope you now see conflicts in a new light – not as problems to be avoided, but as catalysts for innovation and strengthened relationships. By embracing effective communication, empathy, and collaboration, you have the power to create a conflict-resilient workplace that thrives on openness and mutual respect.

Remember, conflicts are not indicative of failure; they are natural occurrences in any dynamic environment. The key lies in how we approach and manage them. Armed with the knowledge and strategies provided in this book, you are well-prepared to lead by example and foster a culture where conflicts are addressed constructively, leading to enhanced teamwork and increased productivity.

As you implement the strategies outlined here, always keep in mind the profound impact your actions can have on the individuals around you. Whether you are a manager, team leader, or employee, your commitment to effective conflict resolution sets a powerful precedent for those you work with. Together, we can create workplaces where understanding, collaboration, and innovation thrive.

I personally extend my heartfelt gratitude for joining me on this journey to mastering conflict resolution in the workplace. As you continue to apply these strategies, remember that every conflict is an opportunity to learn, grow, and build stronger connections. Embrace conflicts as stepping stones to success, and witness the positive transformation of your workplace culture.

Now, it is time to unleash the power of effective conflict resolution and propel your organization toward a future of collaboration, productivity, and success. Embrace the challenges, foster open communication, and let your journey to a conflict-resilient workplace begin. Here is to a brighter, more harmonious, and successful future!

Wishing you all the best in your quest for effective conflict resolution, a harmonious and productive work environment.

9 798859 516247